THE INNER GOD
AND HAPPINESS

PEKKA ERVAST

THE
INNER GOD

AND

HAPPINESS

Pekka Ervast Series
II

Published by Aatma
www.aatma.fi

ISBN 978-951-8995-23-7

Translated by Lauri Livistö
Proofreading and corrections by Ilkka Castren

Cover painting by Hilma af Klint
Photograph by Pirjo Aalto
Preface and back cover text by Pirjo Aalto
Layout by Lauri Livistö

Original Finnish title: Jumala ja onni
Published in 1923

The translation of this book was supported by
the Kulmakoulu foundation.

FOR THE READER

Pekka Ervast held seven lectures between September and October 1922, and based on these lectures he compiled a book called *Jumala ja onni* here published as an English translation as *The Inner God and Happiness*. The content of the book was current when it was first published 50 years after the birth of the Theosophical movement, and it still is so today: People still ask what is the purpose of life and seek happiness.

Ervast shows how the existence of God can be examined through philosophical reflection, and how it is our human responsibility to seek truth. Following open-minded research one may get an experience that God loves one and all humans and other creatures unconditionally. He shows us that after having done away with external dividing characteristics we as a humanity are all brothers together, and we should take care of each other. Life wants us to be happy, but our conceptions of happiness are erroneous.

PUBLICATIONS IN ENGLISH:

The Mission of the Theosophical Society, An open letter to Theosophists the world over (1921)

The Sermon on the Mount , or the Key to Christianity (1933)

"H. P. B."; Four Episodes from the Life of the Sphinx of the Nineteenth Century (1933)

The Esoteric School of Jesus (1979)

Astral Schools (ebook 1979)

The Key to the Kalevala (1999)

The Divine Seed: The Esoteric Teachings of Jesus (2010)

From Death to Rebirth (ebook 2017)

From Death to Rebirth (audiobook 2018)

Spiritual Knowledge (2018)

The Inner God and Happiness (2018)

The Inner God and Happiness (ebook 2018)

www.pekkaervast.net

TABLE OF CONTENTS

I
THE PURPOSE OF THE THEOSOPHICAL MOVEMENT

Now as we begin this winter's work it is time, as usual, to take a look at the Theosophical movement itself. We have always considered specific topics during each winter, but at the beginning of this period it is good to recall what purpose the Theosophical movement has.

If we wish to describe this purpose with a few words, we could say that from the very beginning it has been to stir people up from spiritual lethargy and laziness, to awaken humanity from a too convenient self-satisfaction and meaningless hurrying, to inspire people to think of the grand questions of life, to make them stop in their fuss and bustle and to ask themselves, what is existence, what is the meaning of life? To put it briefly: the purpose of the Theosophical movement is to awaken us to seek truth.

I could then be claimed that truth has always been sought, we have scientific research for that purpose and that is all what it does, its sole purpose is to seek truth. Theosophy will answer to that: the question is not of the truth that can be sought with modern scientific means. It is not about knowledge which in course evolves and expands, which changes with time. This is not about that. For when a person truly begins to think and asks oneself what is the purpose of life, one is not asking for a scientific truth which may vary from time to time. One cannot be content with such an account of life which natural science is able to give, on whatever phase or stage of development natural science happens to be, for natural science explained life totally differently thirty or fifty years ago than how it does now. Natural science and scientific search for truth taking place in universities is changeable. It is subject to change and development. As time passes and its knowledge increases it gives a constantly changing view of the world and the meaning of human life.

Therefore a person who is sincerely inquiring for the purpose of life cannot in one's spirit accept the explanation science can give, which today may be materialistic and tomorrow nobly skeptic. So one asks: Is there no eternal and unchanging truth? Is there no enlightenment and knowledge which would solve the mystery of life and its perennial questions once and for all? Is there no such truth?

Thus asks a human being in one's spirit, and that spirit will only accept an answer which has a feel of eternity.

The Theosophical movement has declared from the very beginning that such truth exists. And it has added the even more significant fact: such truth is attainable. People need not wander in darkness, nor do they have to seek truth only by scientific means, for they have the possibility of finding eternal truth.

Truth can be found – this was the message of the Theosophical movement from the very beginning, its unchanging message. No other movement, no other person in our time nor during recent centuries has dared say anything like this. No other than the Theosophical movement, Madame Blavatsky and her students.

When we further inquire how the Theosophical movement defines this concept of truth, we have an immediate answer in the name Theosophy itself. For what reason is the name "Theosophy" chosen, a word which means "divine wisdom"? The answer is: "truth" in its eternal meaning is the same as "God". But Madame Blavatsky preferred not to translate the word "Theosophy" with words "the wisdom of God" or "the wisdom about God", but she preferred it to be translated "wisdom such as the gods have", that is, "divine wisdom" or "wisdom of the gods".

This may seem peculiar at first. But if we think about it further we will understand how appropriate Madame Blavatsky's translation really is. She wanted to point out that the concept "wisdom about God" is too vague. Anyone can claim to be "God-wise" or to know "God". Such a claim is easily made by someone who believes to have found or experienced something one considers valuable and profound. But not just anyone can say: I have wisdom such as gods have, for practically this means nothing if it is not known what kind of wisdom gods have.

Madame Blavatsky wanted to say that such knowledge as the gods have of truth, of God, is also knowledge, or wisdom, which is obtainable by humans as well. She did not want to claim vaguely that we can obtain knowledge of God. She also wanted to add how much knowledge we are entitled to pursue regarding God which is truth: we are entitled to as much as the gods have.

Some may think that this explanation of Madame Blavatsky's feels somewhat superstitiously exaggerating, for "gods" seem rather fairytale-like legendary creatures. But the more a seeker immerses oneself in the Theosophical understanding of life and the more one finds out what kind of knowledge is attainable by humans, then the more one will understand how humbly did Madame Blavatsky really define this knowledge. So humbly, and yet so thoroughly and exactly. For wisdom which is attainable by humans is wisdom which already exists. What would we know even of the possibilities of attaining wisdom unless there already were Wise Ones? We may call these Wise Ones divine beings, gods, masters, redeemers or use whatever name one wish, their existence guarantees the possibility of obtaining knowledge and wisdom for us as well. The question about the existence of these divine beings is not on today's agenda, but we all know that a core teaching of the Theosophical movement is the very existence of those divine beings.

So Madame Blavatsky made her appearance in the world with this extraordinary message. Her task was to announce and proclaim with vigor and verve for humanity the message that truth could be found, because there were those who knew the truth.

And what was the world like where she worked? Despite the fact that truth was scientifically "sought", the world then, as it does now, flattered itself with the claim that it had already "found out the truth". Obviously the world never admits that it would not know the truth. Humanity would never want to admit honestly that it really knows nothing. Only the most brilliant and ingenious people dare say: "we really know nothing. We would like to know. From where and how could we gain real knowledge?" Only the most ingenious people dare to say this. The world is always so pleased with its idea that it already knows the truth. This is how it was when Madame Blavatsky made her appearance. The thinkers representing natural sciences were assured and established with the idea that the world was "materialistically" made of, and that the only truthful world view was a materialistic one. If God was discussed with them they would say: we do not know about such a thing, we do not understand the whole concept, we cannot see where this God would be. There is no "God". There is no other life than what we perceive around us with our senses. This is what we study and we have found out that it is without "soul", without "God". Everything is of matter, everything is of concrete material substance. Life itself is a grand manifestation of matter. There is the riddle of it, there is the solution of it.

One half of the world was very content thinking and feeling in such a way. The other half of humanity was clinging onto all kinds of religious beliefs. This half said: "we have the truth. God himself has given us the truth." The world was divided into all sorts of religions, and religions into all kinds of sects, and every sect was very satisfied with the belief that they alone had the knowledge of truth. They all protested to Madame Blavatsky: We already possess the knowledge of truth. How dare you suggest that we seek the truth, for we already have that! It has already been given to us. It is in the teaching of our sect. God himself has declared it to us, and we in our own sect have the best understanding of truth. It is an obvious, proven fact that we know best how the revelation God has given for humanity has to be understood!

People were extremely content and satisfied with the belief that they held the truth. Upon closer examination of different sects and religions it became clear that they all had disagreeing and often the silliest ideas of truth, that is, of God. Some believed truth was contained in a specific book, in "the word". Quite a few had an image of God as a terrible tyrant who could cast some poor human souls into "eternal damnation" and torment them there for unending aeons, "eternally". Philosophically speaking we can generalize that the materialists believed they knew that life itself was just a great materiality, an impersonal existence or force which had no feelings, no thoughts, which pitied no one, cared for no one; the religious people had the notion of God that he was a personal creator of the material world, of the manifested existence, a personal ruler who controlled and guided everything. And therefore in different sects it was a general belief that this personal leader and creator favored in special ways the members and individuals of merely "our church". This great and powerful ruler and creator of the world loved especially them. God wished best for them, only them he wanted in paradise after death. But woe to all those damned beings outside their blessed church! Woe to them! The great creator and ruler of the world hated them; hated them righteously for their sins, for their darkness and for their disbelief. They would have no mercy. All the people who had not heard of the sweet message of mercy of this particular church wandered the world in the greatest of perils. What would become of them? God's infinite, dire wrath would crush them and torment them eternally!

So believed Christians in their sects and churches. They gathered together to thank God who was so merciful to them, who let them be saved, although the rest of humanity was destined to eternal damnation.

This was the situation in the western world when Madame Blavatsky made her appearance. It is not exactly like that anymore. It has soon been fifty years since the Theosophical movement was initiated. The world has become a bit wiser since that time. We have progressed somewhat in civilization – a little, not much. So we should not be too proud, we should not imagine that already we would have become noble-minded philosophers. Not at all. There are still many things reminding us of those past times, but we have made a little progress, become a bit more enlightened. We are able to think a bit differently now. We are more careful about our judgments and criticisms. If we belong to a certain sect we are not so hasty to judge others as the children of damnation. We have become aware that it would be too sweeping, too dumb and too childish, – no one really blindly believes that kind of judgmentalness anymore. Humanity has learned to ask: but what about this eternal damnation? Is it absolutely sure that this damnation truly exists?

The Theosophical, spiritistic and other such movements fighting against materialism have achieved a revolution in the understanding and views of people, and the progress of natural sciences too has, as it were, opened the gates for a more spiritual world view. Life is no more considered to be so childishly simple as materialism thought it would be. It is filled with mysteries and secrets. It offers countless phenomena to scientists which cannot be explained materialistically.

Thus the world is more open to spiritual and idealistic views of life than it was fifty years ago. And those views are everywhere around. All sorts of "mystics" and "sages", writers and thinkers are offering their answers to the riddles of life – and are competing against each other for popularity. Simple and sincere seekers of truth would be like seafarers in the night without a compass, unless Madame Blavatsky had not given them in the great basic teachings of the Theosophical movement stars shining in the darkness by which they can guide their journey and search.

So there lies a danger also in the polar opposite of materialism which is pure spirituality. This noble view says: there is no matter, matter is only an illusion. The existence is only consciousness. And what is consciousness? It is God, God's awareness. An aware and conceiving, personal God is the only thing that exists.

This is a very profound and very philosophical view – and especially an Eastern point of view. It enchants many seekers who do not know to be wary. It satisfies them and lures even many who have studied Theosophy. If one does not know what, according to Madame Blavatsky, is the beginning and foundation of all Theosophical search for truth, one may end up in such an Eastern view when becoming acquainted with Theosophical world view. It is attractive to one's soul, but too – how would I say? – religious leaning that it could raise one into that objective knowledge of truth, which will "liberate" one's soul.

I will try to describe this so to speak "Eastern" and quite mystical, quite profound belief about God.

It centers around a conception that behind all existence is a personal consciousness, a great peculiar consciousness, which thinks, or as it may be said in the East, "dreams". What is all this existence?, asks an Oriental and answers that it is some mysterious being, some immensely great and wondrous consciousness "dreaming". The whole existence is only this God thinking, this God imagining, this God dreaming.

This is a very profound view. Even the keenest and most mystical writers could adopt this view, or as Madame Blavatsky might say – get lost in it. And that is not difficult because even according to Theosophy such a being or consciousness does exist. It is the Soul of the World, it is the "logos", which is behind all existence.

We can easily imagine a dreamy Oriental who is sitting and contemplating and envisions that the whole existence is merely God's imagination. And when that person's life is regular and peaceful where nothing really happens, then one considers one's own life too to be only a dream. "What actually is real in my existence?", one asks oneself. "I sleep and get up, I work and I eat and go to sleep again. My whole existence is a dream. And it is not even my dream, but a dream of some great, fantastic being! I am merely a thought of this other being, only a dream image in the dreaming of this other being! There is no reality. This life is not real, everything is maya", like a Hindu would say, "everything is unreal illusion. Everything is a dream."

When does this view suffer a hard blow? When life, which after all is "reality", is harsher than usual, when it confronts the dreamer as an unexpected misfortune – then one really awakens from one's "dream". When the

16

whole world suffers a blow of fate such as for example the World War, then it is difficult for even a dreamer to think that the whole existence is merely a dream, let alone that it would be some other being's dreaming.

But there may also be people, so certain of the unreality of existence, that even if they meet with great sorrows and pain they will still keep thinking that life is just God's dream. However if they go on believing so and if their lives become anguish and they see that life is anguish for others as well, such as in the World War, – then they will add in their mind: the being dreaming all this is in reality an evil being. They will not be able to reason otherwise. They will come to the conclusion that if existence really is a dream, if it is God's imagination, then God is evil. Otherwise why would there be so much suffering? Why else would existence be filled with so much senseless and incomprehensible pain? The one dreaming is a devil.

Here ends the speculation of such a philosopher. The end result is a comfortless fatalism, which in practice can lead weak souls to even tragic consequences, but which, however, as a philosophical standpoint is fascinating.

Therefore this is the first great danger which confronts a seeker of truth as if saying: do not be a materialist but believe in the God which is conscious in the existence, believe in the consciousness which thinks everything into being.

The Theosophy of Madame Blavatsky said: this is a danger, for we should not so suddenly jump into a belief in the Logos as such. We must not think as if we understand the secret of the Logos, for that secret is not the first nor the final secret of existence. Logos is not behind "everything", Logos is not absolute. We get nowhere in our search of truth if we stop like this as believers in Logos. We have to first gain understanding of the absolute life. We have to first reach an impartial and impersonal understanding of life's most profound secret before we can understand any personal mysteries in life.

This is why Madame Blavatsky emphasized in the Theosophical movement as a first principle such truth, which any person could reach who sincerely seeks the truth, who sincerely thinks, who looks at life impartially. Every seeker can reach this truth which Madame Blavatsky emphasized and said: "it is the first consideration. You have to first achieve clarity about this and only then can you understand other mysteries."

What is this truth which Madame Blavatsky gave first priority?

It is the truth about the human being, the truth that we are all humans. What does that mean? It means that we are thinking, feeling and willing beings. And from the perspective of a truth seeker we are above all rational beings asking what is truth. It means that when we as human beings bare and expose ourselves in front of life itself, we have to confess that we do not know the truth. We are seekers, not knowers, – and from this perspective we are all just – humans. But in this visible world we call ourselves with different titles. One says: I am an unlearned shoemaker, and other: I am a learned professor, third says: I am a famous artist, and fourth: I am a mighty king, and so forth. We have to get rid of all these erroneous conceptions. As humans, as truth seekers we are neither poor nor rich, neither learned nor unlearned, not kings nor beggars, not professors nor shoemakers. We are humans, thinking beings seeking truth. This we have to confess.

As long as we imagine and believe that God has favored us by a special grace by giving us some kind of holy book in which we can rely on or by giving us a wise priest in whom we can depend on in spiritual life, in "matters of beatitude", or as long as we believe that by being a king of a great country then surely God will take care of us after death for having already given us such a special and mighty position in this present life, as long as we imagine that because we are popes here on Earth then surely it means something before God – for surely God would not have raised us so high unless we were something special – as long as we believe this we live in delusion. And we have to become free of this delusion. Unless we pass through the gate which strips us bare of our vanity and fallacy, we shall not understand even a single truth. For our first awakening lies in seeing that we are human souls seeking truth but do not really know anything.

In this way we knock on the door of life. For us the door of life is as if the door of heaven. If it opened we would be in heaven. If the door of life would open up for us we would know what life is, what is the truth, who God is. Then we would be in heaven, we would be saved, we would have found what we had been searching for. But as yet we know nothing. We knock.

And when we knock the door may open partially, so that we can see and feel more deeply, know more deeply what life is. That deeper understanding which we gain lies in seeing that we are all brothers. We are all in the same situation. It is of no use being pompous, proud or hypocritical. We are all brothers in this vast, unspeakable ignorance. Madame Blavatsky used to call humanity "the great orphan". The mysterious beauty of this name is revealed to us in that experience. Humanity is the great orphan. How true this is! There is no God dreaming of us whom we could blame, whom we could call the devil. There is nothing like that, for the first truth that we attain a certainty of is only that as a humanity we are like a great orphan with no parents. We are cast here in ignorance. But there are millions and millions of us together – we are brothers. And we who are brothers, we should help each other, support each other! But what do we do? We live like savage beasts, we tear each other to pieces, we argue and wage war. We think we are so secure here on Earth that we can freely oppress and torment each other. We think we are in such good favor of God that we can even kill each other and do whatever evil possible. And when we wage war and condemn others we even call out the name of God and other high beings and try to act in their name. Thus we humans believe and live. So great is our belief in being in the good grace of God.

But when we begin our search for truth then the first truth which is revealed to us is that humanity is a great orphan. We are cast here to get by alone and on our own. We are in no special favor. We are many together, many in the same damnation and we could help each other. And in seeing this our heart bleeds. It screams: Can you not see? We should live as brothers, we should help and love each other. But we are unable to carry out this brotherhood. We are so dumb, so unintelligent, so blind. Actually we are not that evil. In every person there is a human heart. Everyone is a human, if they would only awaken, if they would only come to know themselves, if they only would seek the truth!

And that is why to seek truth is our human responsibility. It is also our only salvation. For as Madame Blavatsky and the Theosophical movement have declared and promised from the very beginning: seeker will find. And the first discovery of a seeker is this brotherhood which is not a sentimental feeling nor a poetic metaphor but a great, terrible and cruel reality which is condemning us all but at the same time liberating us from the illusion in which we live.

II
Is God personal
or impersonal

Let us consider more brotherhood, the grand orphanhood of humanity, but in a way that we ask whether God exists and what is God like? Is God personal or impersonal? If we turn to Theosophy, then it of course will answer: seek truth, seek knowledge about God and thus know that you can reach God, you can obtain knowledge about God.

Is this really so? Are we human beings really able to obtain knowledge of God? What then does the word "knowledge" mean?

To this Theosophy answers: the word "knowledge" in this case means experience, it means knowledge based on experience. Usually the word is used in a broader, more indefinite way. There is for example academic knowledge, which is obtained primarily by reading – and partially by making observations. These academic studies are therefore in the best part book learning, memorized knowledge.

Now Theosophy says that it is not about that kind of knowledge when we are talking about "knowledge of truth" or "knowledge of God". It is not about memorized knowledge, but experience.

So what is the difference between memorized knowledge and knowledge based on experience? There is a difference known by all. Let us take an example.

Let us imagine that we see pictures of London, or any other distant city, all sorts of pictures of the scenery in London, buildings, churches, museums and even films from London streets. Let us also imagine that we read books about London which tell us about the size of the city, what the population is and what kind of buildings there are and how people live there. In this way we can get a good overall image about London.

And this is what we call some kind of knowledge. For if we compare this to a person who has not read anything about or seen any pictures of London, we will see a definite difference. One knows things the other does not. And yet we admit that this knowledge obtained from books and pictures is not experience in the actual, concrete meaning of the word. For if our knowledge of London is based on experience, it means we have been to London. Anyone with experience knows the tremendous difference between knowledge from books and actual experience. Any knowledge from pictures or books is without life, it is in a way too objective, too much outside of us, whereas in comparison if one travels to London, right in the middle of its life, one will immediately understand the difference between actual experience and the knowledge gained from books. An experience is life itself, it merges into our blood so to speak. "Knowledge" from books must be enlivened by imagination, but a physical experience comes through all our senses as living information straight into our souls. It is as if we see, hear, feel, smell and taste this knowledge.

There is a similar difference concerning higher issues, affairs of the spirit, a difference between experiential knowledge and knowledge based on memory.

When Theosophy instructs us to seek knowledge about God, to seek experience of God, it points out that there is an enormous difference between concepts about God and an experience of God. Most people who say that they believe in God and have a worldview as Christianity teaches have created for themselves images of God, world and human being. They believe they have everything figured out, they have read and heard about these things, they have believed in the same way ever since their childhood and they are completely satisfied. But can they say and claim to know from experience that things really are as they believe? No, they cannot. At least most of them have to confess: "We believe so and we think so. We have not experienced it." How could something like that be experienced? people exclaim. How could God be experienced? And yet there are believers who will pause to consider this claim and say: "something can be experienced." They claim to have experienced "something", but cannot explain what it is that they have experienced. They may say for example: "I have experienced the grace of God. I know that God forgives us and we receive reconciliation with God in Christ." But even then their conception is so vague that we would be too intrusive if we harassed them with our questions. They are not philosophical enough to be able to answer our questions. They are in fact intimidated: "no, we must not think about these things! We must not think too deeply about these issues!"

Now Theosophy says that if you wish to set out on the path which eventually will lead to knowledge and experience of God, then you must begin in a certain way. There are two parts on this path to knowledge. The first part of the journey is to purify your reason, your thinking, your mind. It is necessary that at first you should become philosophers in a sense that you dare to think. You must have courage to trust your thinking and reason, be truth seekers in a beautiful way like this. You must not fear disbelief, doubt or hopelessness. You must not fear anything in this. You have to embrace such seeking that you bravely dare to think anything possible. And the very first task you have is to think

23

about the question of God by using your reason as forcefully and precisely as possible. Begin to doubt everything.

Maybe you now believe in God as an almighty, all-wise and all-good Creator. However you have to face the truth without fear. You have to say to yourself: If God has created everything and if there is none other than this one almighty, all-knowing and all-good being, then why has He created suffering and evil? You will see that the answer cannot be mixed with any unphilosophical remarks about the devil or fallen angels or such. If God is behind everything, if God has created everything and there is only this almighty God, then it naturally follows that He is also responsible for suffering and evil. Then you ask, why has He created suffering and evil? And when it is even claimed that people, whom God himself has created, can be persecuted by God for their sins and evil, not only in this life but also eternally after death, then you must admit that this kind of God cannot really be good. The almighty God is then not all-good and you are faced with the problem of evil. God actually seems to be evil. For if He as an almighty ruler can tolerate any being to suffer eternally, He must be evil.

This is only a rough example of how boldly we must reflect the most profound questions of life. At the same time we have to find out what the greatest philosophers and most brilliant minds have thought about God, what they have explained and taught of Him. We have to explore everything and as if choose of it that which can satisfy our minds even if only for just a while until again we find flaw in it in some way and push it aside in search of something new. It may be that we end up in a result that God is not personal but some kind of impersonal force or spirit of life. It may also be that we end up where atheists do, in the idea that there is no God at all. We should not discard even such an idea but instead we have to think even this thought through to its definite and final end. We have to seek whether we are able to find some possible satisfaction even in the idea: there is no God.

When you seek God like this and think about the higher questions of life you may observe that when you come to the conclusion that all definitions of God are imperfect and unsatisfying, you will say to yourself: There is no God. And at the same time you may observe yourself suddenly filled by a sense of joyful freedom, – a sigh of liberation escapes your lips: "oh, I am free from this nightmare. There is no reason to believe in God, it is useless to bother one's mind with such questions. And I could never fathom something like that anyway. Surely there is no God."

Now you will feel as if you are sovereign rulers in life, you feel like kings. There is no judge observing your steps or measuring your actions. You can freely tread the walk of life. You can decide everything as you desire and you will be answerable only to yourself. And you will say: "everything is illusion and all this spirituality is just nonsense fairy tales. When a person dies one dies, – then one is free of everything. What does it matter how one has lived? The point is that one has lived the way one wanted to!" A great joy of liberty will fill you. You feel that life is wonderful.

But beware. After a while there will come suffering or grief and life will not look so wonderful anymore. Then once again you will think and ask: "why does a human being exist? Better not to exist at all, for I do not want there to be suffering and misery in the world. I wish that we could be happy, free and joyful. Why does life come and grasp me in its iron grip? Why is life like that? It is against reason that it is like that. I see no reason in why I meet with suffering, why a great defeat takes me by surprise and why I do not succeed in my endeavors. I cannot understand this." And again you wonder about the meaning of life. If everything was alright then you would settle for it. But when life is agony and anguish you ask what is the meaning of this existence.

Again you are faced with this question. You have now come to the point in your thinking, reflecting and pondering that you confess: "I honestly do not know what to believe. For whether I believe this or that, there is always something that is not right. At first I tried to believe in God in various ways and then I tried not to believe in God. Neither was good. Still I was faced with a mystery, an enigma. Still life rose up before me as a sphinx and said: "You must solve the question of life or I will devour you."

However when you have reached this point we can say that you have purified your thoughts and mind, for that is the first period, the first passage of experiencing God.

We must first be purified like this in our intellect so that we would stand naked, unknowing, powerless before life. This is the first experience we have to have of the secret of God. Let us remember: we cannot obtain any real knowledge until we have purified our brain like this. We must as if sweep clean our inner house. As an apostle said: "Human being is a temple of the holy spirit." This is the first secret. We have to understand that we ourselves are temples of God. So we must cast out of our minds all false idols, all images and preferences and concepts we have of God! We must be rid of them. We have to purify ourselves so that we could become what we are: temples of the holy spirit and not the caverns of thieves and robbers. We must come to the point that we know our own ignorance, that we know only that we are human beings, hearts which love and quiver and would want to experience God.

Then we will see this marvelous truth which I spoke of earlier, the truth that we are all brothers, and not in any external sense, – for then we would only find too many factors separating us from each other, – but in the fundamental meaning that spiritually we are all brothers. We are as if spiritually one in the ignorance which hides from us the secret of life: God. In this regard our humanity really is, as Madame Blavatsky said, a great orphan. We are cast here alone. We wander alone in the world. Humanity is a great orphan who does not know what life is and who lives generations after generations and millennia after millennia, creating history on this globe in space, but knowing not why it lives, and knowing not God who is the beginning of life.

This is the first truth which we will see. We have to experience it in our blood as it were. We must experience it in our soul and spirit. It is not enough that we read about it in a book or hear someone speak about it. We must experience it, and the experience will come when we have exhausted our mind from thinking. Perhaps not everybody will be able to do it. Many who will not find any enlightening literature will have to ask over and over again: who God is, and in the end become mad. One only wonders how many people are locked in our mental asylums just because they have not had answers to their questions. A person like that could be among the most noble and intelligent of people but had no one helping in the days of their struggles. For as Jesus says in the gospels: Those who are called to be leaders of people, those who are Pharisees and have learning sit on the throne of Moses. But instead of opening the gates to the kingdom of knowledge for those who seek, they sit on their chairs in front of the gate blocking the way from those who seek. They have nothing to give from their formal position, they are not able to guide or help those people who come to them in the agony of their souls. And because of that many people lose their minds thinking about these things.

What a great help Theosophical literature is in this regard to the seeker. It helps in one's reflections of these questions, it shows new and wonderful views in

27

which one's mind may rest for a long time. However, sooner or later life will come as a sphinx, reality as an experience, and ask: tell me: who is God? And then one has to answer.

But now that question does not come too soon. The seeker will not be terrified by it. Calmly one will answer: Yes, I stand here naked and ignorant before life. But then one will see and know: all people stand alike in the same situation.

The whole humanity is one exactly like this. Yes, this is our first experience as seekers of truth. We stand as brothers before God – yet without seeing God.

But if we accept and take in this first great solution, we let our hearts as if whisper quietly: we are all brothers. And in this our hearts are reborn. Now we feel that as a humanity we are like a great family. We are one big brotherhood. We are no longer learned nor ignorant, not poor nor rich, not noble nor lowly, not Finnish nor Swedish, not English nor Russian, not socialist nor capitalist or of any party – we are just human beings. All things which separate us from each other will become insignificant, will fade away. We no longer care about them. If someone flaunts before us with their knowledge or high status or wealth or whatever, why should it affect us? Those things are nothing. The person standing there so fancily dressed, who is wealthy beyond belief or learned beyond belief, he or she too is just a human, just as small and helpless before life, just as naked and ignorant as us. Or if someone comes before us so humbled, so small, so poor that the person dare not even look up, afraid that one might offend us with one's insignificance, then we will encourage that person. We know within that he or she is a human just like the rest of us, filled with the same longing, just as mysterious, just as divine.

There will grow in our hearts the rose of life which is called brotherly love. Our hearts are transformed and we will grow to become new persons. We will not become prophets, not renowned wise people, not saints to be lifted atop a glass tower for all to see and admire. Nothing like that. Nothing is seen on the surface – the change happens within us. Do you know? When the heart is transformed and brotherly love awakens in a human, his natural instinct hides this secret, for it would feel horrible if anyone saw or knew what a peculiar creature one is evolving into. Because now one suffers and rejoices in a totally different way than before. If someone suffers even a little so shall one suffer too in ways unspeakable. If someone rejoices, one rejoices with that person. If one sees something beautiful, one will melt in tears; and if one sees goodness one wants to worship.

No, it is something one feels one has to hide from others. One would rather present oneself as a sinner and a lousy creature whom people despise and avoid. One would regard it terrible to reveal to the world that something new and divine lives within one, that one no longer is any ordinary John or Jenny, but instead the whole humanity gradually begins to live inside one, that all those surrounding strangers whom one meets during one's path in life begin to live inside of oneself. One is as if embarrassed by it. One is frightened by it. One does not want to reveal it to anyone. One will conceal oneself.

This is the first natural instinct.

But a new life of brotherly love still keeps growing in oneself. And then something strange happens. As if of itself God will begin to approach one. As if of itself, without one asking for it, one will begin to experience God.

And what will one experience first in the beginning?

One will experience that God exists. Not the God whom one has read about, not the God whom one has imagined about, but God as a reality who will come to one in one's own spirit, in one's own consciousness. It is as if the kingdom of heaven would open up inside one and God is there.

And what is this God? It is God, who loves him or her. Here one does not yet know what God is really. One does not know what God is like, whether God is personal or impersonal. One cannot define God in any way, one only knows that God exists and that God loves him or her.

In time one will notice another thing. One will realize that God loves other people just like him or herself. God loves everybody. "For He makes His sun shine to good and bad alike." For God there is no difference between people, God does not judge personalities. We may say: "oh, how bad I am" or: "I am the greatest sinner of all and you others are all good." But God knows nothing of this – God loves. How will the seeker find out this? We can best see it from an example. Let us say that he or she loves someone. For example a wife whose husband has a dangerous job: a sailor or a pilot, or something like that which is both dangerous and keeps him away from home for long periods of time. The wife who loves her husband is naturally anxious when her husband is at work. Before, when she yet knew nothing of God, her distress was extreme. It was hopeless. And although her husband ensured her: "Do not worry, nothing will happen to me", it only consoled her for a while. For the human imagination is like that, when a loved one is in peril one cannot control the imagination but lives in anxiety and anguish. But after coming to know how God loves her, she will one day suddenly experience that God loves everybody the same. For when she is anxious for her husband, a voice will suddenly speak inside her and say: "why are you distressed? Does your suffering help your husband? Your power is small and limited, what can you do? But do you think that he, your husband, is only in the safe care of your love? Do you think that there is no other protection in life and death?"

And the wife sees that God, who loves her, loves her husband just as much, so that her husband is not in any real peril. She has experienced this regarding herself, that there is nothing to worry because God always loves her. Now she will see and experience that neither her loved ones are in any real peril for God loves them all just the same.

This is truly mysteriously mysterious for God is not any external being who lifts one out of harm's way or paves the road in front of one, or clears away unfavorable winds. Not at all. God is love that exists always and everywhere. There are many secrets in life, but the secret of God is that God as love is always behind us, within our consciousness, within humanity, where we can learn to know Him. This is God.

One who knows God will also soon see that while God is this love inside of us and behind us, God also wants us to be happy.

Let us think about this! What is actually the hardest question for people in life? It is this question: Why are we not happy, why do we suffer, why is life filled with pain and agony? The practical solution to this problem is to see that God wants us to be happy. It is as if God is the second name for our happiness. God does not want any suffering, God does not want any pain. God does not want anything bad. God wants us to be happy. The mystery of existence is solved. For would any one of us say: I do not want to exist if our existence is sheer blessed happiness? Existence is arduous, inexplicable and pointless to us only for as long as we are not happy. But if life is harmony and beauty and loveliness then existence itself has obviously a meaningful purpose and we are satisfied with just that we exist. And then we only ask: Why are people usually not happy? How could they become happy? But then again that is a different question.

III
GOD AND HAPPINESS

When a seeker of truth begins to experience God, the question of whether God is personal or impersonal becomes irrelevant. For him or her God is a living reality and it becomes practically pointless and almost impossible to more closely and accurately define God, to define in a scientifically exact manner whether God is personal or impersonal. Both of these definitions are equally justified for that person. For him or her God is personal because one feels that God is like the other half of one's self, like a Father, like another self whom one can talk to. At the same time God is impersonal because one has no clear knowledge of God's essence and because God cannot be as it were contained within oneself but instead is infinite in comparison to oneself.

One only knows that God is a loving consciousness, love behind oneself and the whole of humanity.

And the deeper one penetrates into the spirit of that loving God, the clearer one understands and sees the wonderful truth which is revealed to one, that God wishes one's happiness, the happiness of all humanity. It is as if God were a will to happiness behind all existence.

Then the seeker will also find out what religions have meant when they have spoken of beatitude and eternal life. Religions have meant precisely that wonderful experience of a human being becoming aware of God. When a human is able to enter into communion with God inside of oneself, then one has become a participant in eternal life and beatitude.

Eternal life does not begin after death. It is futile to think and wait that the eternal life would open up for one simply after death. No. The eternal life does not depend on time or place, it does not depend on casting off this visible body and passing through the gates of death. Eternal life begins at the moment one becomes aware of it. A human being will attain eternal life here on Earth. One has to become participant in eternal beatitude in one's present state.

How many people say: this life is worth nothing. All is meaningless under the sun. All is pointless for everything has already been tried and there is nothing new. For what do we even exist? Would it not be better if we did not exist at all?

And truly: when we look at people, when we stroll the city streets, we rarely see a happy person. We rarely see someone's face beaming with joy or goodness smiling in their eyes. Mostly we see people weighed down by their troubles, tormented by their thoughts, filled with pain, fear and uneasiness.

Despite this and that we see the silent question on people's faces: why do we exist? – despite all that, we see that still they go on with their lives. And what else do we notice deep in their souls? It is as if a voice was sounding in their souls, a voice which promises happiness and harmony, which whispers of a home they belong to. It is because of this secret voice resounding in people's souls that they settle for living their lives which evidently bring them more suffering and pain, trouble and worries than happiness. It is as if people were resigned to the thought of life without happiness, that a person is not really entitled to ask any happiness in life. Young people dream of happiness, but when life confronts them they learn to give up their dreams.

How can the seeker's experience of God as the will to happiness living within humanity apply to all this? Is it possible that God would blindly want people to be happy, but that the living reality would be in conflict with God's will? Or does the conflict depend on us, that we humans have not really understood the whole issue?

When someone experiences that God wants people to happy, then one will also find out why people are not happy. Above all one sees that there can be nothing wrong in happiness that we should be afraid of. On the contrary, we are entitled and called to happiness, eternal life and bliss.

Happiness is attainable by us and we are destined to it.

Then why are we people not happy although God too would want it for us? The seeker will discover the reason to be that we people really do not want to be happy. We do not dare to wish happiness. This is such a strange secret, such a great mystery of life that we must exert our brain and heart for a long time before we understand it. And yet at the same time it is a wonderful truth. Could we learn from those people who have had experiences of God and who know what happiness is? Perhaps, but it is still quite unlikely that simply by hearing what happiness is we would immediately reach it.

The wise people say: "you have an imperfect and wrong idea of happiness." And truly: the idea of happiness is very different with different people. For example let us take some normal people and ask them: do you wish to be happy? They would all answer yes, but when asking everybody separately what would be their happiness, we would get the most differing answers. One would say: I would be happy if I were rich. Another would say: "I would be happy if I was well-known and respected." Then a third: "I would be happy if I had a lot of power and a high office in society." The fourth would say: "I would be happy if the person I love would understand me. I am married and do not ask much from life, but if I could live in harmony with my spouse and if she would love me, I would be happy. Now we just argue and complain about each other and have a difficult life. We have no strength to carry on like this." And other souls have yet more varied wishes regarding life.

And all souls say: "if God has meant us humans to be happy, then surely God has not forbidden our striving to wealth, fame, power, love and so forth. But then why can we not reach those things? Do not speak to us of eternal life and beatitude, we do not understand those things. We do not understand useless religious fantasies. Your God who would want us to live eternal life in eternally bliss does not understand and approve of us and we do not approve of him." – "Give me ten million," says a man who wants to be rich, "and I will be happy, I do not care for anything else."

These souls do not understand God. Their idea of God is of a cruel and remorseless tyrant who does not approve of people's lives. He is "righteous" and wants everyone else to be "righteous" as well. They have an intuitive notion of God that he demands from them something they are not capable of. This is how those souls feel who are honest with themselves. I am not talking about people who organize their lives according to a formal routine, who go to church on Sunday and consider this the way to maintain good relations with this harsh God. During the week they are then "themselves" and care for nothing else but for their own lives.

What do the wise ones say about this? They say: "man, examine yourself. When you learn to know the Father, the God within you, you will also see what is your happiness. Now you do not understand yourself or your real happiness. Do you truly want to be happy? Then set no conditions for happiness. Do not make your happiness depend on anything you have no immediate and natural power over. Do not associate happiness with anything else than God. God wants you to be happy, but you say to God: No, I do not want to be happy, I want to be rich, or: I want to be famous, or: I want to be master and commander."

And what does life say?

Let us examine how life is arranged. Is life so arranged that it altogether prevents us from reaching even that delusional happiness we long for? No, life is not so arranged. On the contrary: life gives us what we hope for so that eventually we would learn to hope for God's everlasting happiness. Life gives whenever possible. I say: if possible, because in the material world material laws apply which slow down the fulfillment of our wishes.

When a human soul wishes love for example, then God who wishes for that soul to be happy says to life: try to give him or her this love. And depending on the flexibility of the material conditions the human soul will sooner or later obtain love.

Here we have to take into account that a human soul is born again and again into the world. The wishes the soul is not able to fulfill now, it can fulfill later. Human being plays with life, one is like a child playing with soap bubbles. One might say: I want to hold this blue bubble in my hands. But it is difficult to reach with one's hands. And if a person wishes for wealth, the wealth will not come spontaneously but only after efforts as a final reward. But what will follow when a person has become rich according to one's wishes and desires – whether one was born rich or has gained wealth in this life due to one's efforts? One has merely caught a soap bubble which immediately burst. One did not become happy. One is just as miserable as before. For a while one thought one was happy because one had gratified one's wants. But already in a while one noticed that one had not gained what one had really wanted, because one had wished for happiness but had believed that happiness depended on wealth. Now one gained wealth but not happiness.

The wise ones say: "oh, human, as long as you define yourself what happiness is and what it depends on, so long you will not reach it. You will certainly achieve something and be pleased that there is some joy and pleasure in life besides just suffering. You will even become philosophical and say that every pleasure has to be bought with suffering, and you will submit to everything – but you will not have gained happiness. And yet you exist for the purpose of becoming happy, but you can become happy only by seeking and finding God."

Life truly is peculiar. When someone has found God and says to Him, like Jesus said: Father, you know what I need to be happy, – then God will give it to one. At one time one's happiness might include poverty and at another time riches, but what is certain is that whatever belongs to one's happiness one will then get. The Father knows how this person who is like a manifestation of the Father, his own son or daughter, will be happy and this happiness will come. It will then come by the will of God, by the will of happiness itself, by necessity and not because the human wants or desires so oneself. When a person neither wishes nor desires anything special, just wishes to be happy, just to be in communion with God, then some strange, mysterious force of life will bring one whatever is necessary for one's happiness. This is the secret of life and I do not know whether I have managed to explain it. But it is a wondrous thing for it makes life a great glorious adventure. And I say: what prevents our happiness so greatly are not the common accidents such as diseases and bodily suffering which usually make us unhappy but instead our own reluctance.

So if God wants us to be happy, then why would He wish us to fall into bodily suffering? On the contrary, if we listen to God's voice, we will hear it say: "I do not wish for accidents, I do not wish for sickness or injury, but you who live in this material world are subject to the laws of the material world. Just understand that I your God do not wish you to suffer and therefore wish as I wish and say welcome to your sufferings. Say: "you cannot take away my happiness. You cannot diminish it either, for you belong to this visible, momentary life. If I have in my ignorance broken the laws of the material world and sickness will be the consequence of it, – then let it come. My happiness lies in repaying my debts and suffering gladly what I have to suffer, and then suffering does not really exist anymore."

When someone has experienced God, one neither fears nor resists suffering. One knows that God wishes one to be happy and healthy and if one is confronted with bouts of evil or difficult times which try to prevent one from being happy, they will vanish and disappear, they are transient, they do not belong to oneself, they are not abiding obstacles to one's happiness and beatitude. One's happiness is beyond time and therefore a time will come when diseases and suffering dare not approach one or people in general.

Then there is yet another issue. "How can I be happy," a human being asks, "when there is so much weakness and so many flaws in me, when I am a sinner and an imperfect creature who stumbles and falls. Do you not, God, judge me for my weakness and failings? Are you not a severe and righteous God?"

The wise ones say: "oh human, listen to the voice of the silence within your heart. Listen to what God has to say." So one listens, and thus speaks God: "my dear son, you have misunderstood me. If you think that I judge and criticize you, then you do not understand my love properly, for I only wish to help you. Why do you speak of your sins and flaws? Are you certain that these sins, failings and flaws really are in you or have you become convinced of it because other people have told you so? Take refuge in me. Imagine that I am a stream of life which passes through meadows and woods and furrows itself through great rocks and meets on its way stones and mire and mud. Take a pause by a shore of that current and listen how the stream sings and the waters of my life resound when they face an obstacle. When the stream rushes against rocks and stones it blows beautiful sounds. You human are such a stone or rock on the path of the divine stream. If there is something in you which cannot stand against me, I will wash it away and then there will be something in you which resounds. Other people are not called to criticize and judge you, for my stream will cleanse you of all the dirt and mud, so that all that is left is a stone which resounds beautifully. Therefore I say to you human: You are safe, look towards me, trust me and fear nothing. Do not criticize or judge yourself so that you would not criticize or judge others. For what do you people know? Why do you criticize each other? You are like judges who see flaws in everyone else but not in yourselves. But I do not criticize, I do not judge, I your God only wish to help and therefore if you are aware of the Father within you, then help one another but leave criticism and judgments aside. And you can help one another ultimately only by believing in God, by believing that I, who am in you, am also in others, that I am in every one of you and wish to make all of you happy. You cannot help one another by blaming and pointing a finger and berating one another, for then you take a moral high ground and set yourselves above others as if better. When I your God am in this sinner, is it right that you call him or her bad even when you know that I am in that person? I walk my ways through his or her form and want that person to be happy. So how can you be proud and criticize him or her? That person knows within that one is not so despicable and bad. So instead go to that person and teach one to believe in me, influence one in a way that one will become aware that one is a part of me. Then one will overcome one's weakness and cast off sin. One will not be able to do so as long as you call one a sinner. But one will become free of it when you help one to find out what is the secret of one's life, when one reaches faith in the possibility of eternal happiness."

And when a human says: "I would be happy if I could be happily in love with my partner. We want to be together and live with each other, but why do we make our lives hell? Is it wrong to wish for happiness?" Then to this God will answer in the seeker's heart: "I want you and your partner to be happy. Do you want it?" One replies: "Of course. If only my spouse would also understand this, would also wish for happiness, for I do so." "No," says God, "it does not depend on it. Your happiness must not depend on your partner understanding this or that. I want you to be happy with your companion just the way one is.""But how is this possible?" "Do you not see," says God, "it is the clearest and simplest of things: want to be happy. What is your happiness? Find out whether your happiness lies in anything else than in the happiness of the person whom you love. It certainly is nothing else than that, for his or her happiness will be reflected on you. Always keep in mind that you are happy when the other one is happy. Make him happy. Do as she wishes. Demand nothing, ask nothing for yourself. Your happiness does not depend on what the other person is like, your happiness depends on you to serve him or her." Thus speaks God inside the human heart.

This is such a profound and strange mystery that although we speak of it openly, it still remains a mystery. For it is true that we cannot be happy without knowing God and when we have reached communion with God, we will constantly live in the present moment, constantly win over and over again in time the happiness which does not originate from time but from eternity.

IV
GOD AND MANKIND

For the one who knows God life is a grand adventure in which one plays the part of a wandering knight. One rides one's horse and journeys towards unknown destinies. But the meaning and goal of one's life is to help those who suffer, console those who weep, support and protect orphans and widows. One feels inside as did a medieval knight who set out into the world to defend all the weak, to oppose all wrong and to fight for all justice.

And yet one need not be a merely sentimental person. One may well be a profound philosopher and a sharp thinker. One does not have to abandon the use of one's reason although one "lives by every word that comes forth from the mouth of God". God speaks to one also with the language of reason, not only of conscience, heart and ecstasy. Therefore as a seeker of truth one does not abandon philosophizing and thinking, but continues it with new vigor. One is not satisfied to say to oneself: thus and thus I have experienced and more I shall not think, but instead one tries to clarify one's experiences to one's reason, to think ever better. Immediately after having had one's first experiences one sets oneself the question of God's relationship to humanity by asking: "is that God which I know to exist the infinite life itself?

Is it the absolute life which all philosophy talks about and all thinking is based on? Is it the absolute reality behind everything? Is this that God? And if it is, then how can I understand that the unconditioned divine life would have manifested in me, a finite being, that this absolute would talk in me and to me, that this infinite, absolute life which is without definition would manifest in this universe? Is it possible to think that this is so?"

When the seeker of truth sets oneself this question, one's reason will immediately comment: can the infinite, absolute life be manifested at all? Or to put it more realistically: can it be in relation to anything? A human says to oneself: within myself I am in relation to God. And the reason asks: is "God" the infinite and absolute life? Can the infinite, eternal, absolute life, divinity, be in relation to a finite being, a human?

Thus our reason receives as if a mathematical problem. We may think mathematically that there are two quantities: infinite and finite. Human would be finite, both in one's mind, for one's mental life is limited, as well as in the body which can be weighed, measured and so forth. Human may thus be compared to a finite number. Is there then any relation between this infinite and this finite? What does our mathematical reason say? Impossible! There is no relation between the infinite and the finite, because the relation is indicated by division, and if we divide the infinite with a finite quantity it will not work. The result is still infinite. So we cannot have any relation to the infinite God, nor can the infinite have any relation to us which we could speak of in any way or which we could define in any way. For the real relation of the infinite would still be the same infinite which is unchanging and does not manifest in any way.

Therefore it is provable by mathematics that the infinite divinity cannot have any relation to finite beings, and thus it is impossible that we would have any knowledge of the infinite divinity.

But if we cannot have any knowledge of the infinite and eternal divinity, then what can we have knowledge of? What divinity or God is then manifested? We perceive before us the manifested cosmos. We ourselves are parts of the manifested God – we have received before in experience an absolute proof of the existence of manifested God. But if this manifested divine life is not the manifestation of the infinite, eternal absolute, then what is it? It has to be a manifestation of something else. Of what? God of course, but then God is something which can become manifest. How can we satisfactorily solve this strange question of God and the manifested existence?

Do we have any mathematical figure or concept which would describe eternity and infinity? Yes we do. Such a mathematical concept is for example the geometric figure circle. Circle describes infinity, for its circumference is unending: there is an infinite line which yet is limited. We can proceed the circumference of a circle for all eternity without ever arriving at an end. And yet it is finite. The circumference of a circle is even mathematically such a strange notion that we cannot specify or measure it quite exactly. We get peculiar calculations when we wish to mathematically state the size of a circle's circumference. We are not able to arrive at an exact number but have to be content with approximate values. We say that the circumference of a circle is π or *pi* times the diameter. But what is this π ? This Greek letter states a value which cannot be measured exactly. It is 3,1415926... continuing as a figure till infinity.

We are not able to measure the circumference of a circle as we would measure a straight line. Practically we can use a measuring unit such as a meter, but then we will not reach the true mathematical significance of the issue. Although they are finite there is something mysterious in circle and sphere, something which reminds of infinity, the absolute life. In a closed circle which as such symbolizes the limitedness of existence lies yet some of the mysteriousness of the infinite and the absolute.

In a similar way we can also say that if we compared God to a circle, a sphere, then God could become manifested. Even if we could not define God any more closely than we can mathematically describe and measure the circumference of a circle, God could still in this case become manifested, just like spheres exist in reality, just like our whole existence on this planet and solar system is in a way a manifestation of spheres with circumferences.

This takes us to the Einstein's theory which has recently gained attention with scientists around the world. Although I am not very familiar with it, I know that it claims that our manifested world is not infinite but finite. This is philosophically and at least according to the occult philosophy the absolute truth: infinity cannot become manifested. That which becomes manifested is finite. Even if our universe were infinitely big or as the French astronomer Flammarion so poetically says that "even if we traveled across space we would never reach an end, we would always be at the center", – no matter how huge our universe is – and it is impossibly vast, we can prove it astronomically and mathematically – it yet could not be infinite. It must be like a sphere, like a circumference of a circle. It must be infinite in a sense that we may travel along a single line as far as possible, forever, without reaching any end. Any other type of infinity we cannot understand with our reason. Infinity itself cannot have become manifested, but that which manifests is an image of the infinity which we can symbolize with a sphere. The manifested infinity is like a mirror image of the unmanifested infinity. The amazing possibility of manifestation lies in infinity, and we can describe it with the circumference of a circle, or in practice with an infinite unending line.

In all profound occult philosophy it is said that the manifested God which "exists" and "creates the world" and is seeking itself in its own creation, is Logos, Number, Reason, Word of which it is said in the gospel of John that the "Word was with God and the Word was God." In the Gospel of John there has been made a philosophically valid separation between God as the mysterious infinite and Logos as the manifested Word and it is added that: "God was the Word". The purpose of this addition is to point out that no matter how clairvoyant and spiritually evolved we were, we still could not fathom anything else than Logos, the manifested God, which nevertheless is on its other side the same as the all-containing and all-embracing infinity and non-existence behind everything and of which we can say nothing else than the Hindu philosophic phrase: "Neti, neti – it is not this, it is not that." We can do nothing else but negate any limited qualities from the unconditional absolute. But the manifested God, Logos, is that which represents as in a mirror to our human reason the mystery of God – just like the circumference of circle mathematically and quite realistically describes infinity and eternity.

We arrive at the same view of God by another way as well. We reach a bit more intimate and – how would I put it – more vivid and tangible, less abstract understanding of God if we begin from the other end, – not from the abstract infinity which is God, but from ourselves and our experiences. Ancient sages have stated as a rule which is absolutely true that everywhere in existence prevails the law of correspondence. And so there is a short proverb from ancient Egypt: "as above, so below", which likewise means also: "as below, so above". In other words the saying holds a truth that when we wish to study that which is above, then let us study that which is below. We need not start from that great, miraculous life which to us is a secret and which we say is everywhere around us and of which we are only a tiny, insignificant part, but instead we may begin precisely from this tiny, insignificant part, from ourselves and then by carefully examining ourselves begin to understand that great life and the mystery of the manifested God. But for this it is almost necessary that we first have some experiences of God, and then afterwards use them as a basis and ground for our reflective thinking. Although it is basically always good to reflect, our thinking nevertheless moves as if in an empty space, without a basis, until we have experienced something. When we have experienced God it is as if our thinking then had a home built high on a rock from which it flies out to study the world but always returns to its home to recall what is the truth and in light of the truth to evaluate what it has seen on its expedition.

Now when we examine ourselves in a realistic, everyday manner we find ourselves to be manifested as these corporeal beings. And because our bodily existence is so familiar and so easily perceivable to us, there are many people who say that there is no other existence at all. Although they must admit that they have thoughts and feelings, wants and desires, the whole of what we call psyche or life of the soul, they account it all to the bodily construction. Materialists have tried to explain that thoughts originate in the brain through a chemical process. It is true that our thoughts, mental images, experiences of the soul are mostly born through sensory perceptions. We have either seen or heard, or for example read something from a book, and based on such sensory perceptions formed ourselves mental conceptions, thoughts. With such mental imagery we then operate within our consciousness. But if we claimed strictly like the materialists that there can be no experiences outside physicality, that our whole existence as spiritual beings is completely dependent on the physical organism of our body, we would go too far in our claims. Then would be left unexplained many experiences of soul and spirit which dumbfound materialistic minds.

We cannot delve now into all kinds of so-called supernatural phenomena, but I would like to point out one psychological issue which fits our subject and is also a difficult problem to solve for materialistic thinkers. When a materialist says: all our mental images and thoughts have been born through materialistic sensations and have thus formed our so-called soul or soul-life, we ask: What then causes it when a truly worldly person who has enjoyed worldly life and has been a great "sinner" like pious people would say, what brings it about that this person suddenly awakens and reaches an understanding of God or higher inner life and abandons one's sins, pleasures, selfish deeds, and turns about, changes and begins to live a new life? What causes this?

If the materialists are somewhat philosophical and scientifically-minded, they will point out that it is not certain that the transformation of the person would be permanent. The whole "conversion" can well be a superficial, momentary state of soul brought about by some sensory perception or passing experience. The person in question has been in a "revival meeting", received a powerful impression through one's senses which then has caused an "awakening" or a "conversion". But how long will this last?, the materialists ask. We answer: let us not immediately talk about its duration or presume that it lasts – but how do you explain the phenomenon itself? This will make the materialists think and say: well, of course this conversion could not have happened so abruptly. There must have been some kind of preparation for it. Surely this person had previously had guilty perceptions which criticized him of bad and selfish living and aroused thoughts of improvement. Of course one had experienced such things for already some time. This is how our materialists will answer.

But we say: you have explained that every thought

and all mental images one can have come through one's perceptions and that one operates in one's consciousness with these images. But if this person who "awakened" has never knowingly had such mental images, then how do they influence him or her? At first the materialists become slightly confused. But then they remember that these days there is a lot of talk about "subconsciousness". People receive a great deal of sensory perceptions which do not reach the daily waking consciousness and of which they are not aware. We walk down the street and see many things in passing to which we pay no attention. We do not remember them but images of them are stored in our subconsciousness. Now the materialists say: this person having awakening has also received many such impressions which influence one without one knowing it. So, we reply, they affect within that person, one is not aware of them, but they still influence within that person? They do, as it is said, in the subconsciousness. So what kind of consciousness is it? Where is that consciousness? How is it possible according to your materialistic view of life that any such subconsciousness even exists? Now the materialists are really confused. They see that they have been digging the ground from beneath their own feet. The most primitive materialism has already been abandoned these days. Now they are parallellists and phenomenalists.

We need not stop here but let us take a historical example: St. Francis of Assisi. Here we have an Italian youth, born in a wealthy home, handsome – he has all life's good opportunities ahead of him. He lives the happiest of lives with his friends. Wherever people are rejoicing and enjoying themselves, he is always there, he sins a lot and does many thoughtless deeds, he throws himself into the whirl of life as deep as possible. And suddenly – not when he has become old and worn, but in the middle of the prime of his youth and strength – he receives a revelation of something divine and sees that the life he has been living has been delusion. He feels that as a human he is not called to that but to a wholly different kind of life. His mission in life is to follow Christ. At this moment he makes a firm resolution of conversion. Without hesitation he steps on a new path from which he never falters. He begins to live a new ideal life, such that would be lived only after thousands of years, a wonderful, fabulous life of love.

Now we ask the materialists: how do you explain this? What bodily circumstance caused this? Was his body special, was it organized in a different way than the bodies of other people? Surely you do not claim that St. Francis was a pathological phenomenon, that he was an exception from the normal humanity, a sick degenerate being? You would not dare to think of that, even less to say aloud. Not even the most hardened materialist could believe that the loveliest and most unselfish, beautiful life that ever has been lived on Earth would be a pathological phenomenon.

Even he gladly admits that such a life as was St. Francis of Assisi's is much more beautiful than what we usually live. A being such as St. Francis of Assisi is above regular people, more spiritual and more evolved.

When our materialists admit as much as this, could they not also admit that there must be something else in a human being besides just one's thoughts, feelings and expressions of will which originate from one's sensory perceptions? We believe and know that there is more to a human. There is something which can inspire one from within. Within one there is an internal, invisible, immaterial life, one is a spiritual being, a soul which makes one an inhabitant of another, spiritual, invisible world just as one lives through one's body in the visible world. One's thoughts and feelings do not originate solely from one's body but as a soul, as a thinking, feeling and willing self one receives inspirations from the divine world of the spirit.

I would like to mention what the extrasensory perception of a human being as a soul is like. It is in fact very peculiar.

In this visible world a human is a limited, corporeal being. The outlines of one's body are all curved but one is still not a sphere. The body's characteristics can be measured accurately. One is an objective creature in this visible world. But the same human is in another world, seen with the inner eye, a sphere. As a soul one is spherical and as such a symbol of the infinite divinity. As a spiritual being one is God manifested because one is a circular sphere whose circumference cannot be measured.

Thus seen from this level human has an inner, unmanifested world, there is something divine in one's being which can inspire and influence the physically manifested person.

Therefore occult philosophy, as does mathematics, speaks of the quadrature of the circle, squaring the circle. In occult philosophy it is said – and every Qabbalist knows this in practice – that if someone wants to understand and know how God manifests, then one has to solve the quadrature of the circle. He has to know how to square the circle.

What does this mean? Mathematically, in geometry, it naturally means that one has to draw a square which has an equal area with a given circle, or to create a cube which has an equal volume with a given sphere. This, as we know from mathematics, is impossible because we are not able to calculate exactly the circumference of a circle in real numbers. With algebraic numbers it is of course definable: the circumference of a circle is $2\pi r$ and the area of a circle is πr^2. But in practice we cannot calculate this exactly. Therefore the quadrature of the circle is a mystery. It remains unsolved whether it is possible to draw a square which has exactly the same area as a given circle has.

However it is said in occultism: if you want to understand the relationship between the Logos and its world, the manifested life, then you have to understand the quadrature of the circle and cubing of the sphere. And this is not impossible in practice because God, existence, nature has solved this question. As souls we are circular spheres but in this visible, manifested life our form is a cube and this has also astonishing symbolism.

If we fold a cube out of paper and then open it and spread out all of its six sides, a cross will be thus formed, a typical christian cross. The cube is a human, and when one spreads out one's arms, one is a cross.

In the visible world human is a cross or cube, and as a soul one is a circle or sphere.

Thus we reach the first macrocosmic analogy: when human, sphere as soul, is manifested visibly as a cube in the form of a cross, so accordingly we can understand that the world is a manifestation of the circular spherical Logos in the shape of a cube, thus squaring the circle and solving in practice the mathematically impossible problem.

But now we face an important question: is this sphere that we are as souls, is it the only God we can become aware of? Do we know merely ourselves when we know God within us? Do we become aware only of our own sphere?

By asking this question we expand on vaster horizons, take on new roads. We take yet another step closer to the mystery of God, we ask yet more light to our thinking and inquisitive reason.

The inner God and happiness

V
LOGOS AND MANKIND

When one who knows God uses one's reason and intellect then one will say to oneself: I know that I am in touch with a mysterious, divine life and that this divine life manifests within myself. But what is this divine life? Who is the God whom I know? How should I understand my wondrous experience?

One will naturally admit that the experience cannot originate from one's corporeal life nor from one's ordinary mental life, but that it must instead originate from somewhere much deeper. Because experientially one only knows and feels the inspiration which is a living reality within him or her, one will say to oneself: Is there something in my being which can be called divine? And then one must admit to oneself that purely empirically, based on one's experience, it is true that there is something within oneself which does not originate from the body nor the ordinary mental life and which in itself is without a parallel in physical and mental life.

But when the seeker of truth comes so far in one's philosophical reflecting, one as if becomes frightened and stops. No, one says, it cannot be so that it would only be my own soul. No, I am aware of something which is outside of my whole being, which is far greater than myself, far more wondrous and sublime. I cannot limit and narrow it down within my own soul.

There are psychologists of religion who have halted here when they have studied the religious soul-life of other people. They have studied it as precisely as it has been possible for them based on accounts and literary notes and they have come to the natural conclusion that behind it all is inspiration which comes from a mysterious hidden origin within the human soul. It is not possible to reach any further than this in the examination of the phenomenon with scientific, objective means. The furthest they can go is to say that the human soul is greater than the daily waking consciousness, just like modern psychological research has reached the conclusion that the human soul-life is divided into daily waking consciousness and subconsciousness.

But as we already pointed out, the seeker of truth, the knower of God, is not satisfied with such an explanation that one would be in contact merely with one's own self, one's own soul because one clearly feels that the inspiration has come from outside of oneself. It now depends on one's temperament whether one will stop here or whether one wants to understand more. One could say: "I cannot delve deeper into the secrets of my soul, I have to assume the same opinion as every other regular believer who has found something and is content in one's faith. I too will settle for the inner experience and knowledge that I am in connection with God". So one becomes a mystic.

One devotes oneself to living a divine life in one's spirit and does not demand any more clarity. One believes that in a way everything is already clarified, for one knows God to be one's father and all humans to be one's brothers and sisters. What else would he or she need? Such is the temperament of a mystic.

But there is another, more discerning and reasoning type of character who insists on understanding and comprehending. It fears that it will be led astray – either to doubt too much or to believe too much. It is unable to settle for a peaceful faith which does not seek nor inquire, but instead it asks: has no one ever felt and experienced and lived these things before? And if someone has, then how did he or she solve the problem? This kind of character we would call the temperament of an occultist.

The occultist is a realist in one's own field. A mystic can be a dreamer and work in one's spirit with unproven ideas, and they will not disturb or harm one's inner life. But the occultist wants to avoid as much as possible empty speculations, false notions and ideas. One wants to deal only with realities, facts and knowledge based on experience. Just like a person who wants to know something about India will not fantasize pointlessly, will not think that people are blue and walk upside down. No, one will either travel oneself to India or read and listen to what those who have been to India can tell. In the same way the occultist avoids empty speculations and lures of imagination when one is reflecting the great question of life. So although one has one's own experience of God on which one's meditation can be founded, one yet wants to heed what the sages with a lot of experience in divine affairs tell of the great mysteries of life. Thus one works with true and real mental images in one's consciousness and accordingly one's philosophizing will not be empty speculation, but fruitful meditation which will help one in one's personal life.

Let us now presume that our seeker has the temperament of an occultist, that one wants to explore the sayings and teachings of the sages and occult researchers. What will one hear then? Learn to understand your inspiration, say the sages. Notice that there are many kinds of inspiration. Learn to differentiate the sources of different inspirations. There is higher inspiration, and there is lower. Knowing God is based on high inspiration. Therefore learn to know the scale of inspirations and their functioning! Do not begin by thinking too highly of yourself. Remember that all people are similar to yourself. They are all souls and therefore greater than their waking consciousnesses. What is it really that separates you from most other people? The fact that most people do not know that they are greater than their waking consciousness. Most people believe that they are merely what their waking consciousness is, but you know from experience that in reality they are something far greater. Now look at people. Do you think that their lives are spent solely in external sensory perception? Do you think they never have any inner inspirations? If you do you are mistaken. All people will undoubtedly say that they also have inspirations from within. However they are not such inspirations that would cause them to be born anew for the rest of their lives, but they are smaller. They listen to beautiful music or watch a beautiful play and become enthralled by it. They vibrate, they receive energy. Their inspiration lasts only for a while but leaves a feeling state which in time weakens and dissolves. Now you have to learn to differentiate where each inspiration comes from, because everything depends on it.

It is true that people mostly receive their inspiration through their external senses, but can we really say that it is merely this sensory perception which inspires, invigorates and empowers? Because it is merely a formation of an image in consciousness by these perceptions, whereas inspiration as a source of power has only its beginning in that perception but is a transformation which comes from within, a change in one's state of being which is primarily a psychological but also a physiological phenomenon ("intoxication"). What is this internal transformation? What causes it? Where does it originate from?

Observe now, say the sages, that this psycho-physiological transformation, this inspiration originates from the invisible world and its multitude of forces. Your own subconsciousness is in the invisible world and by reacting to external stimulation rises above the level of awareness. It is an important factor worth noting. But it is not the only one. The invisible world is filled with forces who await like batteries filled with energy to release their charge through your subconsciousness. They are for example the dead, spirits of nature, gods, angels and so forth.

There is an infinite amount of the dead, and not nearly all of them are in a state that their presence would awaken only high inspirations in the souls of the living people. On the contrary, as it is with the spirits of nature, their influence can be very downward dragging and stimulate selfish desires, provided there is a resonance to it in the living counterpart. The religions speak of people being surrounded by "temptations" and "allurements", of which the greater part is of the lower kind, because they originate from the dead, who yet have not been purified of their lower essence, but spend their time within Earth's sphere, either in "hell" or in "purgatory".

On the other hand it is true that the dead who have risen from their degradation, been purified and have ascended to "heaven", are in a different position. Their inspiration is of the same quality as is our so-called conscience. They live in our conscience and influence us positively.

Likewise is the case with angels and gods. They teach people to understand beauty, to see harmony in shapes and colors and to hear it in chords and melodies. They inspire above all artists.

Rather peculiar godly beings are the so-called guardian angels of different nations, the national spirits, or national devas. Sometimes they are also called racial gods and because their influence on people is very extensive, we will say a few words about them.

When a large group of people live in the same country forming one nation, their personal thought and emotional fields merge into the invisible world which is surrounding the country. This forms the so-called national spirit. This national spirit consists of the atmospheres of the souls of all the living and dead. It is truly a greater energy battery of which every person is a part as a smaller battery and with which everyone is in constant connection, so that the collective national spirit can influence a person inspirationally in a most profound way. The most heartfelt emotions can be awakened in a person by appealing to one's patriotism, to one's nationality and one will then be much more unselfish than one would be as just an individual, and therefore we speak of the love for one's homeland and of the national feeling. It is a profound emotion and it elevates us beyond ourselves. Its inspiration is so powerful that it will even lead us to die for it.

What is it in this national spirit which affects individuals in such a great, nationalistic way? Is it just the sum of the experiences of individual personalities? No. Behind the national spirit is a particular center of consciousness which lives in the national spirit and to which the national spirit is like a personal body, just like the personal psychological content of every human being is the personal body of one's soul. This is the national spirit, deva, guardian angel whose influence through the national spirit to the individual human beings is immeasurably strong. With an invisible ruling hand this spirit binds a great amount of people together. If a nation is in danger, a strange love and a sense of connection awakens in all the individual people of the nation, and this will greatly demand them to forget themselves and to fight, to live and die for the common homeland.

Only a knower of God will be free of its power if it were to lead to hatred towards other nations, because he or she receives one's inspiration from an even greater source. One who knows God stands deeper in the stream of life, for one sees that all humans are brothers and sisters, no matter what nationality they belong to. One's God is the God of all of humanity, who knows all humans to be His children, regardless of race, color, nationality or anything such.

Therefore his experience is the greatest. It does not come from the national spirit, but from the consciousness which contains the whole humanity. It comes from the consciousness which is called the Logos and with another name as Christ. The one who knows God receives one's experience from Christ. In Christ all the souls of humanity are united forming a grand mysterious body in which is draped the Logos of humanity, Christ. It is the body of Christ. As souls, as spiritual beings, as individuals we are like cells in the body of Christ, and when we receive inspirations which awaken brotherly love in us and show us our common Father, these inspirations originate from the Logos of humanity, Christ.

VI
INDIVIDUAL HAPPINESS

If we claimed that the purpose of life is to be happy we would probably win only the youth over to our side. Young people believe in happiness, in seeking happiness and the possibility of reaching happiness, but older, more "experienced" people would immediately object to our claim. They would say: "the purpose of life cannot be in reaching happiness. We know that happiness cannot be reached." And if we asked them why happiness would not be possible, we would get two kinds of explanations and answers to our question. Those older people would be as if divided into two groups. The other group would explain that becoming happy is impossible for the simple reason that they themselves have experienced it so. Happiness is a like a winged wheel which flies out of reach just when you think you have grasped it. The other group would answer: "just think about it. Could it be possible that the goal and purpose of life would be individual happiness when at the same time humanity consists of thousands of millions of individual human beings for whom happiness is not possible? Humanity will not become happy by the efforts of separate individuals striving to be happy. On the contrary it would be selfish and wrong of the individual to hope to be happy when the greater part of humanity is unhappy. If we could suddenly change life here on Earth to be a paradise for all people, then we could say that happiness can be reached. But because this is impossible, it is also philosophically and morally wrong that a few people would be happy when the rest of the humanity is not. All people mostly suffer from troubles, hardships, agonies and sorrows – then why should a single person be happy?"

What can we say to this? In these talks we have followed the life and spiritual experiences of a seeker of truth, so let us ask how he or she would address these claims.

One's findings have indeed led one in the direction that would support the claims which were just mentioned. The wise sages who have traveled the path before oneself and whose observations one has learned to trust, for all that one has experienced spiritually has proven their greater knowledge, – these sages have taught that humanity forms a great spiritual whole. Just like the body of a human being is composed of cells, there is a kind of spiritual "body" of humanity in which the cells are individual humans, and this spiritual body of humanity serves as a vehicle for humanity's great collective consciousness which is behind all people and all humanity. This consciousness we call either Logos, or Christ, or God. It is this great collective consciousness behind the whole humanity which is as if a sense of self in this collective body which consists of all individual selves or spirit-souls of people. Therefore when the knower of God either believes in this collective unity as a philosophical truth which the wise sages have explained or knows it to be true based on one's own internal supersensory understanding, then one will ask oneself: "is there after all not a contradiction between the inner voice of God and the collective unity of humanity? The inner voice says: you should be happy. But how can I be happy as long as humanity in general is suffering? How should I solve this conflict? God says I should be happy, but my reason and understanding tell me that we are all one, so that it actually is wrong and impossible for an individual to be happy."

But when one is asking this of oneself the answer will also occur in one's mind and solve the problem. One only has to listen to the voice of God within and at the same time think of the unity of humanity, so that one can clearly see how the conflict vanishes and in fact a harmony is born between these two opposites, the order of God: for the individual to be happy and the suffering of humanity. Because when one thinks more closely about the unity of humanity, its great spiritual body in which one is a single cell and one's own relationship to this collective consciousness which is behind and within every individual consciousness, one will soon understand something. The relationship of individual humans to the internal collective consciousness, their relation to Logos or Christ, is not at all the same as is the relationship of physical cells to a human consciousness in a human body. What is the difference? The difference is that the individual as a human soul, the human as a spiritual being is never far from the center point, never far from the collective inner consciousness of humanity. Every single human individual is just as close to this inner consciousness. On the other hand the cells of our physical body are not immediately near to our personal consciousness. On the contrary, we as humans have a rather vague and distant connection to all the cells of our body. Our waking consciousness is not in any immediate connection to the cells and organs of our body. Only when a part of our body gets ill, hurt or irritated, we know it exists and troubles us. When one is healthy one really does not even consider too much of the composition of one's body. One merely feels lightly that it is there as a totality. Therefore our consciousness is far from the cells of our body, and the cells of our body are also far from our consciousness. This is a considerable difference, for the consciousness of Logos or Christ is not far from any individual human consciousness, but on the contrary every human individual is inside this consciousness of God which embodies all the human individuals as souls, as spiritual beings. And yet most of them know nothing of this Christ with which they are in direct contact. They are in the same position as are the cells in our physical body which know nothing of the great consciousness behind all the cells. But whereas our personal consciousness in the body is far distant from the consciousness of the cells, the Christ consciousness is close to every human individual. The only thing that is needed is that the human heart, reason, conscience would open up to God as a flower opens to sunlight so that the Christ consciousness could descend into a human, would take one over, lift one up. We become aware of our bodily cells only when they are injured or become ill, and then we only want to become free of the disturbance, to be well. Our consciousness does not descend into or unite with the consciousness of our cells, we just receive a message saying that something is wrong. But the consciousness of Christ constantly stands at the door of the human heart, waiting for one to open up one's heart to God.

When the seeker thus understands that one is not merely some distant faraway cell in the body of Christ, but instead within the body of humanity one is a cell which is as close to the center point or the central consciousness as is every other cell, then one's whole problem will be solved. Then God's command within oneself to be happy will become clear. It is not an enticing prompting nor a special favor. It is a command. One's duty, one's mission is to be happy, for in what condition is humanity? Humanity is sick. This great body, the body of Christ is sick. All its cells are sick. If it were healthy, it would be in perfect harmony, every cell would be in harmony together and in direct contact with their inner consciousness, Christ. But humanity is suffering, it wanders in the valley of sorrows, it is as if in a hell of agony here, its individuals wander in ignorance and agony of sin. All kinds of diseases, all kinds of troubles generated by life and nature surround each person. The whole humanity is sick. And God says, the Logos within humanity says: I want you to be healthy and happy and blissful. But can this happen by any sudden trick of magic? Can the whole humanity suddenly become healthy, be free of suffering, illness and all other troubles, agonies of soul and difficulties of sin? No, it cannot. What is the only way humanity can become free of its suffering? The only way is that the cells of humanity, the individuals, one by one, gradually become well. There is no other salvation for humanity. There is no other way to fulfill God's will, to follow the inner demand of Christ. Happiness is not a reward promised after long arduous struggles, but it is the purpose of life. That is why God within us says: you have to become happy, blissful and healthy, for then you will bring happiness and health to all humanity. Then you, as a cell in humanity, will radiate from yourself happiness and health. Is there any other way?, God smilingly asks from the seeker, do you know a better way? Humanity's happiness increases from your happiness, but if you do not want to be happy, if you run away from happiness, then when can humanity become happy? When would my will for humanity's good be fulfilled then? We get nowhere, says God within us, if you do not become my helpers, if you do not wish to be happy.

For us truth seekers this whole question is revealed in a new and different light. And then we will understand where our happiness lies and what it is like. We have earlier spoken about how one should not place any limitations nor definitions on happiness. One should not say for example: in order to be happy here on Earth, I must be poor. Nor: in order to be happy, I must be rich. Nor: in order to be happy, I must renounce everything: beauty, joy, happiness. Nor either: in order to be happy,

I must get everything life has to offer.

What then should we say? We have to say thus: our happiness is that we have all the happiness life can offer us. The whole world will be ours. This reminds me of what a wise sage has said: I have conquered the world, the whole world is mine. The whole world obeys and serves me. I have everything that I need to be eternally beatific.

The sages say this, but they have not said that we have to be wandering beggars or be kings on a throne. On the contrary, that is only of secondary importance. They have sat on the thrones of a king, and probably more often have been beggars, like Buddha or Jesus, but they have been happy, for they have had the whole world, they have had all that they have wanted. They probably would have had mere troublesome inconvenience from royal thrones.

But if we were to mistakenly believe that happiness lies in that we outwardly give up everything and wander around, we would soon see that this is not happiness. And on the other hand if we believed that happiness lies in owning a thousand million dollars or in sitting on a king's throne, we would find out that this is not happiness either. Happiness lies in that we find God and that we are in contact with the inner spiritual consciousness of humanity, Christ. The sages say that our happiness lies in feeling that we are the whole humanity, not just a single cell in the body of humanity, but a "microcosm" which is a perfect image of the great world, the macrocosm. That is our happiness, to feel that we are one with the spirit of life.

Here is a significant point in the secret of happiness. Our God says: all that you need and wish to be completely happy and beatific shall be given to you. Now if someone claimed: I have been in contact with God for a long time and still one has a lot of suffering and anguish, the spirit of life would answer him or her:

you have not experienced enough. There is too little faith in you.

And now we reach in fact the final secret of happiness. How is happiness possible and how is it ethically justified? Only in faith. And what is faith? Faith is a bridge between our individuality and the divine consciousness. It is a bridge which must not let become broken. We must have faith. Without faith we cannot be happy. And notice: by faith we do not mean belief in any creeds or dogmas, but instead the inner spiritual life whose foundation is laid when we awaken to know God the Father. Faith is a practical thing. It is faith in God, faith in the consciousness which is one in all of us and which makes humanity one great whole. It is faith in Christ, it is faith in the spirit of life which wants us to be happy. When our faith is weak we are not able to live in a way that we would be happy. But when our faith is strong, when our faith is true and powerful, then are we happy.

How does this faith then manifest in our life? Does it help us here in our visible life? Will it help in our troubles in our everyday life, will it free us of our financial problems, hardships and labor, will it free us from diseases and so forth? What do you expect me to say? Maybe you think that I will say no, but I say: yes. Our faith will free us from all of our cares and troubles and illnesses. Does this mean that we would never have any financial problems, as we always have now, or any sicknesses or other troubles? No, it does not mean that. Or actually I have to admit that I believe it means this too. But it does not mean it would happen immediately.

The only way to be free of illnesses, beginning from the common cold, the only way out of troubles, including financial ones, the only way to be free of vices, including persistent lapsing to weaknesses, the only way to be free of feeling lonely, including the strongest of desires to be loved, the only way to be free of these is faith, faith in life and the purpose of life. It is the only thing that helps in everything. But how does faith manifest?

It manifests either in prayer or in meditation. One person lives more in one's feelings, another reflects and weighs. When the first one has faith, one prays. One has to have a conversation in prayer with one's God. One lives in a strong emotional connection with one's inner Father, one tells Him one's personal issues, reveals to God the deepest secrets of one's soul and altogether stands like a child before one's Father. Within one's soul one is constantly kneeling, because one always feels to be in the presence of majesty.

Another person does not feel inclined to pray, so one meditates. Not a day goes by without one sitting down in peaceful meditation. At least once a day at a certain time one meditates on one's responsibilities and tasks, reflects how one should be as a person so that the bridge of faith would not be broken, how one could travel through life so that one's life could be of help to other people. This is how one meditates, for one's temperament is more quiet, not so passionate, not so emotional.

When a person finds God, one will find out that one's life is like a piece of fabric which one weaves. Here one sits and weaves, what kind of a cloth will it become? Would one want the fabric to be ugly or that it would be beautiful? Because faith has awoken in him or her, one would want it to be beautiful. One wants that one's life would be a great divine adventure, that it would be like a fairy tale of love and happiness.

One believes in this and works for one's faith. Faith lies not only in that we pray and meditate, but also in that we work and do what we can. An old Greek saying goes: God helps those who help themselves. Of course it can also happen in a life of faith that when in great distress a person says to God that one needs this or that, and the help will come miraculously. One has then tried everything and only when one has run out of means, one has surrendered oneself to God and said: if you do not help me now then I am lost. And then something resembling a miracle has happened.

This is the new and wonderful life which begins for a person when one reaches communion with God in one's inner spiritual life. When one has found this inner God, one will know that all happiness that is possible for him or her in the world will be his or hers.

VII
HAPPINESS AND KARMA

Let us imagine that we would visit a seeker of truth, a person who says that he or she has found God, and we would say to him or her: "you have explained to us that a human's task in life is really to become happy and live in happiness. Although we admit that a younger person might dream about life like that, one will not think like that later in one's life. What causes this? Why is it that we people do not really believe in happiness and bliss? What causes it that if we try to find happiness, we do not actually find it? And what causes it that most people do not really even search for happiness?"

If we ask the seeker this, what would he answer?

He would say: "the fact that people do not believe in happiness, that they actually do not even dare to seek happiness depends partly on their ignorance and partly on their lack of courage. People do not have courage to live like they could live."

This is how one who knows God will answer us. And when we ask for a more precise explanation, one will answer us: "see, human being is here on Earth as if a visiting stranger. It is very difficult for one to get by here as one actually should, if one knew what one really is."

Then we ask: "how can we get to know ourselves?"

And our sage will answer: "It will take place in the school of life, through reincarnation". The school of life means that we are here not for the first nor last time, but instead we will come here again and again to learn to know ourselves. And this school of life is not a random institution without laws. We do not end up here randomly to live, experience and die, and randomly reincarnate back here again. The school of life is a precisely arranged institution of learning. When we are born again on Earth, we will continue from where we finished in the previous time. Our new life is a direct consequence of our past. In the school of life there prevails the so-called *law of karma*, the law of justice and balance, which means that no effort ever goes to waste. If we try something, if we strive towards something, this effort has not gone to waste, but will create a consequence, a fruit, which we someday will reap. We do not act in vain, we do not experiment in vain. When, while living here on Earth, we manage to understand something deeply, it is a victory to us as souls, as spiritual beings. Our observations and experiences will become our inner knowledge. If we have made an error with something and then noticed our mistake, we would rather not make the same mistake again. In our current lives we may forget our experiences and make mistakes again, but when we have moved beyond death, our experience, our observation, our lesson will be immersed in our soul and it will become an instinctive ability. So that when we are born again on Earth we have an inborn knowledge of how not to act. Our former mistake has turned into our conscience. Our conscience is born from our previous errors, observations and experiences. Therefore its voice tells us what is right and what is wrong, not to mention that as spiritual beings we are so close to the divine reality that it also has a direct influence on our soul as an ethical guidance. But the voice of the divine reality could not be heard in our personal consciousness if we did not have conscience born of past experiences. Our conscience which is an ethical product of our past evolution is like a channel or a door through which the divine reality can influence us. But our ignorance is so great that we are born dozens, hundreds of times into this world before we really begin to learn to know our innermost self. In humans there is a hidden yearning for happiness and an instinctual knowledge that nothing else can really satisfy one but eternal bliss and peace. But as one is not clearly aware of that, then in one's seeking for happiness one will reach out for everything that is expected to deliver happiness. We have covered this search earlier. Sooner or later one will find whatever one seeks – wealth, glory, power and so forth – but one will not find permanent satisfaction and peace in that.

But we know that when a person has become a bit wiser, he will as if gather his animal-human strength and say to himself: "happiness lies in doing our responsibility." And that responsibility is precisely defined. Because a person is always born into a specific class of society, one's path in life is already defined in it. When one fulfills this responsibility one is happy.

This is a view of life shared by many and in a way the best, most serious people. They say: "life is necessities. Life is compelling. We are compelled to fulfill our obligations. We need not look for any happiness. We do not have to dream anything of life. When we fulfill our obligations, the result is that we are happy." And they will of course say the word "happy" in a specific tone of voice. Yes, of course "happy", for happiness does not exist as in dreams. "We feel calm and satisfied and that is our happiness." This is how very many people think. This is how people who have experienced life feel.

But it is peculiar that if such people do not awaken during their lifetime, there will come a moment when nearing death, as death is already working its way, when they as if awaken to see and understand: "Oh, but life is so much richer and more wonderful than I imagined! Why have I been so blind? Why have I been striving and exhausted even the last of my strength to do my duty? I have been totally mistaken about life. How could I have had so little faith that I did not trust God who is behind everything and who has meant this life to be something special!"

Such an awakening will come to those people too. They have been good people in their life and have fulfilled their duties. Their conscience is clear and they are not afraid at the moment of death. On the contrary they are filled with peculiar joy and feel that they are leaving to God's peace. But at the same time they see that they have not understood life.

Let us consider other type of people. There are people in whom the inner voice of life has become somewhat heard. They do not have to be aware of this, but within them the force of life resonates in a noticeable way. Such people are either artistic souls, or scientific souls, or true religious souls.

What is characteristic of an artistic soul? It is that it loves life itself and does not want to define it. Artistic soul seeks and tries to see beauty everywhere. A true artist does not wish to define life and to say that it should be like this or that, but instead one studies life. One examines what life is like. One looks at all living beings as works of art. One admires them all. One is delighted by everything. Artistic soul does not understand any division between good and evil in a way they are defined: "This thing is moral, this is immoral, this is good and this is bad, this is right, this is wrong." – one understands no such things. Of course one understands what other people mean by such judgments. But one cannot look at life like that. One thinks that someone who is said to be "an immoral creature" or "a great sinner" is just as fascinating as someone who is said to be "a model citizen". One feels that all people are equally interesting as they are and would not even think of saying to someone: "you should be like this", and to another: "you should not be like this". Instead one especially admires the fact that people are different. For him or her every person reveals life's mysteries, explains life's meaning. For him or her every person is a new work of wonder.

Such is the artistic soul. It would not be able to understand people and see the beautiful in the midst of ugliness if it were not "liberal-minded" like that. Impartial admiration is the deepest quality of one's soul. One sees beauty everywhere and teaches us to understand beauty with one's paintings, compositions, poems, acting and so forth. One sees more beauty in nature and in life than we ordinary people because one's eyes are free from prejudice.

And it really is worth it! Other people who are not able to be like an artist move through life as if they were in some kind of shop where the shelves are filled with bottles and jars and everything is labeled. And they say of a bottle: "so, this is poison." And of another: "this is sweet jam." This is how they define each other. They are not able to admire all like artistic souls. They are not free of prejudice. And therefore they do not understand the artistic soul either. The conventional world will readily label an artist to be sinful for one enjoys the company of "all sorts of people" and sees all kinds of good in every person.

But although the world does not understand an artistic soul, he or she is such a person in whom the spirit of life has begun to whisper instinctively.

What then is philosophical or scientific soul like? This type of soul cares about nothing else in life than truth and knowledge. One wants to know. One wants to see the truth. But because one is a thinker, one does not explore in the same way as does the artistic soul who goes out to the world of experience, but instead one seeks and wants to understand the laws of life ruling all phenomena. One is a true philosopher. One is unable to consider the practicalities of the external world. One is unable to properly consider oneself and how one is dressed. It does not concern him or her what one looks like. The artistic soul on the other hand likes to dress beautifully, originally and distinctively. Especially in the old times artists were known for their willingness to stand out from other people by their outfits and their behaviour. The more comical they appeared to the world, the more artistic they were to their own eyes. But the philosopher, the scientific thinker does not even remember to consider such things. One completely ignores such things and may go about dressed in a most careless way. One may even look like a fool and yet one is not aware of it oneself. One is like an innocent child. One is not interested in anything else than the great ideals and thoughts seen through the intellect. When one discovers a law of nature or a law of spiritual life, one rejoices. Then is one happy and joyful – one sees the truth. This type also is liberal, if allowed to be oneself, much more liberal than the world at large. One is not prejudiced and does not judge people in the same way the conventional world does. One considers people as sovereign individuals in this great intellectual riddle of life. All are living beings, equal, just as good. One does not grade by appearances. Therefore a true thinker, a scientist, just like a true artist, can be easily fooled in the matters of everyday life. Their weaknesses are exploited by the devious and evil people of the world.

And finally, what are truly religious people like? Many people who consider themselves religious or of whom it is said that they are religious are not always so. People can be mistaken about other people, and they can be mistaken about themselves. We have only one certain and absolute sign of a truly religious person in whose soul the spirit of life speaks as a religious instinct. Such a person admires and strives above all towards goodness and justice. One pursues all virtues. If someone is truly religious, one instinctively admires everything good and right, everything unselfish. It is easy for him or her to understand the idea that there is God who rules the world. It is easy to believe that there is behind life a divine will who wants us humans to be good, pure, simple, humble, just and so forth. One feels that all should share these virtues for one feels them in oneself. A truly religious person could do no wrong. One could not be evil, one could not be knowingly selfish. The characteristic feature of religiousness is the love of goodness. If we think about the great founders of new religions they all teach that we should give up selfishness, evil, sin, wrongdoing and strive towards goodness, justice and so forth. The instinct of a religious person always leads towards goodness.

If the religious instinct is not vivid enough in one, so that it would completely permeate one's mind, if the voice of the spirit of life sounds only weakly in one, then one is not able to be good. On the contrary one's inner conviction of the need to be good often makes one cruel and demanding in regard to other people. Therefore we cannot count this kind of people among the truly religious. They are not yet souls in whom the spirit of life speaks in a religious way, but instead they are ordinary everyday persons who in the course of their lives and in societal conditions come under religious influences so that it may be advantageous for them externally and societally to pretend to be religious, go to church, listen to sermons by priests and so forth. Their religiousness is not real. The influence has come from outside of them and something in their souls has echoed a response. But this is so small that it yet does not make them religious souls. We have to keep this difference in mind when we want to understand a truly religious person.

Now we may see that some artistic, thinking or religious souls, or other type of people as well, have reached a peculiar point in their souls' inner life. They are no longer filled with the force of life, active enthusiasm, faith in life. They are tired and ask themselves: "what is life? Is it worth anything?" Nothing satisfies them. "Life would be something if I had enthusiasm and faith – then it would be worth living. But I have no faith. This life feels meaningless. Better not to exist at all. I had better cease to exist. The best solution for life, the most wonderful and lovely would be not to have to exist at all."

In fact everyone will reach this point sooner or later.

And what is this? At what point is a human being then?

One has then reached a point of which the greatest helper of humanity says: "the kingdom of heaven is at hand." If one can truly honestly say: "I have no faith in anything, least of all in myself and my own happiness; now I want to cease to be", and if it is not a passing physical weakness nor a result of exhausting one's life forces to a great work or something else so that one would feel only momentarily empty, then there shines the common Buddhist teaching sweet in one's mind: "nonexistence is the solution to everything. All existence is sorrow and suffering! Strive away from existence! Strive for nonexistence! Strive for the ending of all, to nirvana!" And here many may believe that the Buddha really taught so, – Buddha was the wisest of all. A tired soul may not observe that if nirvana is nonexistence and the Buddha had reached nirvana, then how is it that he was still existing after reaching it? He traveled around India for forty five years and preached: Strive for nirvana, strive to fade out, strive for nonexistence. And yet he himself, who taught this way, existed. Even he could not show by example that his teaching was true. Even he himself could not prove its validity. Is there not a contradiction?

There would indeed be a contradiction if the interpretation of this negative mood of the person in question would be right when one says to oneself: sweetest would be nonexistence. But that interpretation is not correct and therefore the Buddha's words have been misunderstood, perhaps somewhat even in the Orient. For the nirvana of which Buddha taught was of course something a person can reach in one's lifetime, because Buddha said: I am in nirvana, I have reached nirvana. Therefore nirvana means rather the same as Christ's words: the kingdom of heaven is at hand.

When someone has reached the point where one feels morally tired, what is one tired of really? One is tired of oneself. One is tired of one's personal existence. One is tired of selfishness. Selfishness has become a heavy burden to the person. And even if one's selfishness was infinitely subtle, even if one could not get a hold of one's selfishness, one would still feel an oppressive burden with one's sense of self. So when Christ comes and says: the kingdom of heaven is at hand, it only means: "human, give up yourself. Renounce your personality. Your selfhood you do not have to give up. That which says "I", the subject in you, you cannot renounce. But everything that says: I am this or that, I am like this or like that, all that you can and you have to give up in order to gain life, that is: the life of the kingdom of heaven. Life is life in the kingdom of God. Life is eternal bliss and peace. Life is happiness and joy. This life begins when you give up yourself, cast away all your worries and say: here I am. I no longer want to define life. Now I just wish that the spirit of life would totally fill me, so that I could obey the will of the heavenly Father in all of my existence. This is how I wish my life to be. I no longer make any demands. I no longer say: Life should be this or that to me. I give up all that. I just say: If I only could serve life! If I only could fulfill life's will!"

When someone understands this, then one is ready to receive the kingdom of heaven. One is able to see as if in a vision what one's life's final destination has to be. He or she has to become a pure manifestation of life, a servant of God, a child of God, a son of God. And in order to be able to be that completely, one has to reach perfection. Therefore the kingdom of heaven says to one: "the time is at hand, do not miss your opportunity." People wander almost for too long in darkness and ignorance. People are so stubborn. We want so badly to decide for ourselves how things ought to be. If there were courage and wisdom in us we would say: "here we are! Let Life, God use us!" If we dared to set out on this path our happiness would begin, our eternal life, our peace and bliss.

Let us now imagine that we would begin to live life this way, that we would say to life: take me, make something of me, use me in some way! Would we immediately be able to perfectly live this new life? No. But we are here in this world precisely for the reason that we would learn to live perfectly. All life we have previously lived is a preparation for this, a hint of this. But one must have courage to completely surrender to life, to God, when one begins the new life of the kingdom of heaven. Although one is not yet able to live in a perfect way one has nevertheless "set out on the path". And life will say to that person on the path: "everything that you are, set it at the service of life. Every person has some kind of talent, as Christ said, some kind of ability, some kind of tendency towards some particular work or activity. Now set it at the service of life. Do not think of yourself. Use your ability, as it is said in religious language, for the glory of God." And life adds: "do only the work that you love. Do no other work for it is only the work you love that you can give to the service of life. Artistic souls and thinking souls and other similar souls are slightly ahead of the rest of humanity, for they love. They love life. They love their own task in life, their own work. Therefore know this: any work that you love, do just that, for that is work you can do for the glory of God. You need not intervene in other people's tasks. An old oriental saying goes: the dharma or vocation of a given person is filled with dangers for others. Even if it were easier to you or would bring you glory, do not do it but instead let each person carry out their own dharma, their own life task. You carry out your own. Put your strength and vigor and soul into it and do your work for the sake of life and for the glory of life. Then you will be happy."

Let us think about the youth, let us think about people who stand before life and who should choose a direction and calling for themselves in life. The conventional world is all too eager to say to those young people: "this and this is what you should do. Your whole family has done such work – you too should do that." How eager is the conventional world to define how the young people should build their lives. From the point of view of life itself this is all wrong. The world and other people, parents, if they wish to be wise should say to the young ones nothing else than: "do what you love, what to you is highest, most beautiful and loveliest, even if it were in our eyes small and insignificant! No matter how simple work you do, as long as it is to you great and ideal, we will bless you."

We actually raise our youth and children in a totally wrong direction. We cultivate all kinds of prejudices in them. We raise them away from truth and life. We estrange them from ideals, goodness, beauty and truth. We raise them to think what they should and should not be. But instead we should raise them so that they would feel and know that the greatest thing in life is to see what is each one's calling at the service of life. And when a young person's soul opens up to see an ideal, we should respect that ideal. Thus demands life.

Life will place all of us in that kind of point.

We have to place our work and calling to the service of life, to use our talent like that. Each time we are born in the world we are given a calling. This mission becomes greater and more demanding by life if our soul becomes accustomed to doing what echoes inside it as the voice of life. If we fulfill our mission for the glory of life, we advance on the path which leads to perfection, to perfect happiness and bliss and peace.

From the moment a person enters into life's service, into God's service, from that moment on one will be happy. One's happiness has begun then. One is not afraid that the so-called karma sets obstacles in one's way. The obstacles are first of all within oneself: one's own weaknesses, shortcomings, inabilities. Others are outside of one: all the difficulties life sets which are consequences of one's own past actions, one's "bad luck" in life which is a consequence of the past. (Or one's "good luck" in life which can also be a dangerous karma.) All these obstacles, inner and outer, which life throws in one's way, are then part of one's happiness. All is good and happiness when a person has received the kingdom of God. One no longer sees evil, no misfortune, no suffering, in regard to oneself. All of one's sufferings are good because they are all in one's "karma".

And what is karma? Karma is our old debts. Now what has to be done to old debts? They have to be paid off. But the paying of debts is dismal and hard work when we are poor. When we are miserable in life and everything is gloomy – it feels awful and pointless to fight against our weaknesses, to try to overcome ourselves in one respect or another! How hard all this is! We lament and complain that we have such a bad luck in life. Nothing works out. Everybody is hard and callous towards us. Everything is difficult when we are poor. And we are poor indeed as long as we do not know what life is. No wonder it is not pleasant to pay off all debts, that karma feels difficult. Karma throws for example a sickness upon us. Is that fun? No, it feels awful. Although we are being explained that it is karma and now we have a chance to pay off our debt to life, it still feels heavy to us. Although we believe it is karma, we do not feel happy. We bite our lips and remain silent, but we cannot rejoice because it is unpleasant to pay off one's debts when poor.

If we have a big debt and in hard times all our income is spent on living, so that when it is time to pay the debt's installments and interests we can only take more debt, then that is not fun! But how different would it be with our economic affairs if we suddenly received a hundred million in funds! Think about it: a hundred million! It would then be fantastically happy to go to the person from whom we have borrowed our debt: "Here is my debt to you, and I will add a hundred percent interest out of pure joy." If we suddenly become rich the paying of debts feels good, it is then nothing in our large fortune.

A person is in a similar position when one receives the kingdom of God and comes to an internal relation with the spirit of life and truth. One is at the same position as is someone who has suddenly received a hundred million – or much more, an infinite fortune. And when one is so impossibly rich then how could one be anything else than happy and grateful for even the paying of debts? For what are they anymore to one? What are sufferings anymore? One is so rich. The debt means nothing to one. One's soul is filled with joy and happiness and bliss and peace. The sufferings, misfortunes, humiliations, they are all sheer happiness to one.